Basic Christian Magical Theories and Exercises

Albertus Crowley

Published by Albertus Crowley, 2022.

While every precaution has been taken in the preparation of this book, the publisher assumes no responsibility for errors or omissions, or for damages resulting from the use of the information contained herein.

BASIC CHRISTIAN MAGICAL THEORIES AND EXERCISES

First edition. October 21, 2022.

Copyright © 2022 Albertus Crowley.

ISBN: 979-8215808412

Written by Albertus Crowley.

Also by Albertus Crowley

Watch for more at https://www.charlzdelacruz.com/.

Table of Contents

For Hannah

Introduction

Basic Christian Magical Theories and Exercises is an esoteric manual that reveals the magical theories and practices of Christian occultism and mysticism. If you want a Christianity that is pure, genuine, and deeply spiritual, then this is the book for you.

Basic Christian Magical Theories and Exercises is not only a book of information, but it is an invitation to a wonderful adventure—a journey that is overflowing with divine magic. Many witches and sorcerers these days are turning to Christ for a deeper spirituality. The sad thing is that although there are many people who claim to believe in Christ, only a very few are able to penetrate into the mysteries and actually experience the divine presence and wonder of being with Jesus Christ.

Many so-called Christians these days are only Christians by name. Their lives, particularly how they live, usually differ. But, we always have a choice: we can be just like them or we can genuinely and sincerely follow the Divine Master, Jesus Christ. Indeed, there is a huge difference between those who claim to believe in Christ and those who actually follow in the footsteps of the Master.

Basic Christian Magical Theories and Exercises will teach you the essential theoretical knowledge that you need to understand what magic is from a Christian perspective, and you will also learn helpful exercises which you can use in your daily life. After all, Christian magic ought to be experienced on a deep and personal level, and not only to be understood by the intellect. Always remember that real magic is an experiential art. You must experience it personally—because that is the only way to realize and know what it really is.

When Jesus was born, it is written that He was visited by the three magi. It is worth noting that the term *magi* is the plural form of the word *magus*. And, *magus* is the word where the term *magic* came from. As you can see, when Jesus was born, He was visited by three magical practitioners (the three magi). Magic, in and of itself, is not a sin. Just as a knife is neither sinful nor holy. It depends on how you use it. Christian magic uses the art of magic for good and good alone—always in the service of God.

Are you ready now for a magical adventure? If yes, then let me now welcome you into this mysterious and infinite universe of Christian mysticism—where there is true faith, hope, love, and divine magic!

Understanding Christian Magic

There is a big misunderstanding regarding the practice of magic, especially among Christians. Many Christians quickly judge the practice of magic as evil due to having so little spiritual understanding. In fact, these same people do not even know what magic is really all about.

So, what is magic and how is it associated with being a follower of Christ? Magic is quite a tricky term. The reason for this is that magic has various definitions. But, here is something that you must understand: magic is as meaningful as you make it.

For starters, magic is a spiritual path. The acquisition of supernatural powers is only a part of real magic. Always remember that magic is, first and foremost, spiritual. Therefore, the practice of magic should help make you a better human being, and it should elevate your soul. If your practice of magic is not doing this to you, then you are practicing magic in the wrong way.

Christian magic is of a high caliber. This is also one of the reasons why many magical practitioners are now shifting to Christian mysticism. This form of practice is very genuine, sincere, and passionate. It is also an ancient practice, so you will not have to worry about its authenticity.

Christian magic is magic that is based on the teachings of Christ. You will harness the God-given powers of the universe to do the will of God. The primary objective of Christian magic is the same as in mysticism—and that is union with the Divine.

When you do Christian magic, you serve Jesus Christ. He will be your Master. This is actually a good thing, and it is beneficial for you since He is the Divine Master of the universe. It is a well-established teaching that Christ fills all things, for all things were made through Him. He is the Alpha and Omega, the Beginning and the Last. He is the Divine Eternal and the Lord of lords.

When you practice Christian magic, you will never be alone again because Jesus will always be with you every step of the way. This is another reason why many witches and wizards are now turning to Christ as their souls yearn for something real and deep—a meaningful spirituality.

Still, the best and only way to know and understand what Christian magic is all about is through personal experience. Since you will be working directly with God, you can rest assured that it is the path where everything is possible. Indeed, there is no limit to Christian magic, and it is also the spiritual practice that will fill your heart with love, joy, faith, and serenity.

Know the Divine Master

The first step to Christian magic is to get to know the Divine Master, Jesus Christ. Fortunately, this is now easy to do. You can easily acquire a copy of the Christian Bible and get to know Christ. Do not worry, you do not need to read the whole Bible. If you are a complete beginner, it is recommended that you start out by reading the Book of Matthew. The Book of Matthew also happens to be the very first book of the New Testament.

If you are not familiar with the Bible, then know that the Bible is a collection of various books. It is divided into two main categories: the Old Testament and the New Testament. The New Testament is the period of Christ's time here on Earth. However, it should be noted that Christ is also present in the Old Testament, even in the Book of Genesis which happens to be the first book of the Old Testament. Indeed, Jesus is the Alpha and Omega, the Beginning and the Last. He is the Eternal and Divine God.

Going back to the Book of Matthew, it is actually a short book, but it will allow you to learn about the life and teachings of Jesus Christ. I was able to finish reading it in one sitting, and I am sure you can do it, too. After all, the contents of the book are really very interesting.

By simply getting to know Christ, you will be more connected to His divine energy, and this will naturally allow you to feel His presence in your life. Yes, unlike with other gods in the occult where you need to do intricate and complicated rituals just to call them, Christ is always very present, and He wants to have a good relationship with you. He is the One True God who loves you eternally. In fact, even before you get to know Him personally, He has already loved you to the point that He took human form and suffered and died for you. There is no god in the whole history of the universe who has done anything like this for you, except only the true savior, Jesus Christ.

Do not rush your reading of the Book of Matthew. Be sure to pay attention to the story, especially to the teachings of Jesus. It is also strongly recommended that you read His story several times. In fact, the practice of Bible reading should form part of your daily life. In this modern world, it is very easy to be misdirected and manipulated, it really helps to remind ourselves every now and then of the divine teachings, and a good and effective way of doing this is by reading the Bible.

Do not worry about having to read the whole Bible. Indeed, the Bible is a thick book since it is a collection of many books. Do not worry, Christ is not asking you to read everything all at once. The important thing for now is that you get to know as much as you can about Christ. Thanks to technology, this is now very easy to do since you can easily do research online, and there are also many free bibles online or even in the form of an ebook or a downloadable Bible application. Of course, it is always a good thing to have a real physical Bible with you.

It is worth noting that getting to know Christ through the reading of the Bible is definitely very helpful. However, it is not the only way to know Him. Just because you have learned His life and teachings does not mean that the path has come to a close.

But, on the contrary, once you learn about His teachings, then the real adventure is just about to begin.

Mystical Reading of the Bible

As a follower of Christ, reading the Bible should be a part of your daily routine. It should be noted that there are two main ways of reading the Bible. One way of reading the Bible—which is also the most usual way—is by reading the Bible as it is. This means that you would read it as you would any ordinary book or written material. You take the words at their face value. This method of reading the Bible, which is also how the majority of the people read the scriptures, is known as the Antiochian method.

There is nothing wrong with the Antiochian method, and you will still benefit from your Bible readings if you use that approach. However, in Christian magic and mysticism, there is another method that we use, and this method is known as the Alexandrian method, which was put into practice by the desert fathers and mothers in the desert of Egypt long ago.

So, how does the Alexandrian method work? The Alexandrian method transforms the Bible into something much more beautiful and personal. The key to applying the Alexandrian method is to see the Bible as a metaphor. You do not need to see a certain character just as a person or a place to be merely a place. But, rather, you can use your imagination and look beyond things. For example, in the famous story of David and Goliath where the small David was able to kill the menacing warrior, Goliath, you can view Goliath as your most feared and troublesome problem in life. This time, you are David. Know that with the help of God, you can conquer whatever problems and challenges that may come your way.

When you use the Alexandrian method, you use the Bible as a tool to help you internalize the stories and make them intimate and personal. Another good example would be the stories of the various healings made by Christ. As you reflect on the stories, see and feel yourself as one of those people who need healing, be it physical or spiritual healing, or even both. Know that regardless of your personal circumstances in life, you can be sure that Jesus can and will heal you.

The Alexandrian method allows us to have a deeper engagement with the holy scriptures. It might take some getting used to; but just keep on practicing, and you will surely get the hang of it soon.

It should be noted that both methods of reading the Bible are very much helpful. If you are reading a particular story for the first time, then it is good to use the Antiochian method. After all, before you can apply the Alexandrian method really well, you must first be familiar with the actual story that you are reading. A good practice is to read a particular scene several times using the Antiochian method. Once you are well acquainted with the story, then you can easily shift to the Alexandrian method. This way, you get the best of both methods. Just give this approach a try and see how it works for you.

There is another way of reading the Bible that must be given focus on. This approach is also known as the Ignatian way of reading the Bible, as taught by Saint Ignatius. This approach is closely related to the Alexandrian method of reading the Bible. However, you can think of this as a step higher. This approach makes liberal use of the imagination. To do this, you will read a particular scene in the Bible. The first step is to familiarize yourself with it. After several readings, it is time to meditate on it. Close your eyes and imagine the scene happening right now. See and feel yourself within the scene. You may think of yourself as one of the disciples or even a complete stranger who is merely passing by. Use as many senses as possible. Do not just see the scene unfolding in your mind, but you should also feel the air, smell the grass and trees (if there be any), and be completely present in that moment. You can even talk to Christ, if you want. Be fully absorbed into the imagined scene. Remember that God is the God of all things, including the realm of the imagination.

Allow your imagination to run wild and have full reign as to what happens. It is possible that the story may not unfold exactly as written in the scriptures, and that is alright. It would hardly be an adventure if you already know everything that is going to happen.

By using this approach, every story in the Bible will be more meaningful to you. They will resonate with more life and grace. It will also allow you to experience the stories in a way that is personal and intimate since you will be taking part in it as if it was happening just now for the very first time. Just give it a try and see how it works for you. The more times that you do it, the more that you will develop your skills, and the more powerful the experience will be.

Mystical Meditation

We will now discuss a very important practice, which is meditation. If you are truly serious about having any real spiritual and magical progress, then regular practice of meditation is a must. There are many ways to meditate. Do not worry; you do not need to learn all the meditation techniques out there. This is because all meditation techniques lead to one and the same path, which is the path of magical and spiritual enlightenment. It is also good to note that regular practice of meditation will naturally develop your overall psychic and magical faculties.

Contrary to what many people think, meditation is actually very easy to do. In fact, it is so easy that it is more about not doing anything than having to do something. When we meditate, we just have to be still and let go. Especially in this modern world, people are often bombarded with so many thoughts and stresses of the world that it is not easy to find a man who is still and calm. When we meditate, we stop being manipulated by the world. Instead, we just become present in the moment and let go of everything else. It is during this moment that you will experience the magic of the universe unfolding right before you and within you. In this stillness, you will be able to feel the presence of the Divine.

So, how exactly do you meditate? Again, there are countless ways to do meditation. The meditation technique that you are about to learn has been in existence for centuries and was also practiced by the desert fathers and mothers of Egypt. Hence, you can rest assured of its efficacy and authenticity. It would not help so much to keep describing meditation since the only way to understand it is through actual experience. Having said that, here are the steps:

Assume a comfortable position and relax. Close your eyes and do not think about anything. Let go of everything. Just relax and let go of all things and thoughts. Let the mind be clear and at peace. If thoughts arise in the mind, ignore them.

Now, begin to say the following mantra gently and repeatedly: *Maranatha*. This word is in Aramaic, which is the language that is believed to have been spoken by Jesus when He walked the earth. It means, *Come, Lord, come, Lord Jesus.*

Gently focus on your mantra. At first, you may have to whisper it. But, as you go deeper in the meditation, you can stop saying it for you will be able to hear it from within you in some kind of an inner voice. As you focus on your mantra, just stick to it in exclusion of everything else. When thoughts arise in the mind, even if they appear to be important, just ignore them. Now is not the time to think, but this is the moment to be still and relax. Just let go and let Christ.

As you continue, you will soon enter into a deep state of mind. Do not expect for this to happen. Instead, just let everything happen naturally on its own. Do not try to control anything. Meditation is about gentleness and peace instead of force. Do not try to control or force anything. Simply let go and enjoy the meditation journey.

You can end this meditation at any time by gently shifting your focus to your body. Once your awareness is back to your body, slowly move your fingers and toes, and very gently open your eyes. It is important that you return to your body slowly. The reason for this is that if you are coming from a deep state of mind, returning to your body so quickly can cause a bad headache; therefore, be sure to return to your body slowly and gently.

As a basic rule in magic, one should meditate at least twice daily. Take notes that this is only the minimum recommended practice. This means that if you can do more than twice daily, then by all means do so.

Meditation is a spiritual pilgrimage. The mantra that you use (the word that you focus on) is the vehicle that will lead you to your destination. Just keep going forward, and you will surely reach your destination soon and have union with the Divine. In fact, you do not even need to reach the destination before you enjoy the benefits of meditation. It is even possible that you may experience peace of mind on your first attempt to meditate. But, in case nothing seems to happen after several attempts, do not be discouraged. Just keep on practicing. Jesus will also be pleased as He knows that you are constantly asking Him. Moreover, it is not your power that will give you peace of mind, but it is all the power of God made manifest in your life and being.

On Energy

In the practice of magic and many other esoteric arts, you will surely encounter the word energy. This energy is very important because all things are made of energy, both visible and invisible. It is also referred to as life force, while others call it the breath of God. It does not really matter what you call it, but what is important is that you know what it is and that you are able to harness its power effectively.

It should also be noted that this energy goes far beyond the current understanding of conventional science on what energy is. As a practitioner of the magical arts, you must know that this energy is of a divine origin. It also cannot be killed or destroyed, thereby making it eternal.

This energy is pure and divine. It is transmuted from one form into another, but it does not die. Fortunately, even conventional science is now discovering and affirming this nature of energy. Still, as compared with magical wisdom and alchemy, conventional science as the world knows it still has so much to learn.

This magical energy or life force is capable of many things. In its unharnessed state, it usually remains neutral and is directed only according to circumstances. However, in the hands of a skillful magical practitioner, this magical energy could do so much more and so many wonders.

The good news is that it is easy to manipulate magical energy as long as you know how to do it properly. Here is a simple exercise that you can do to have a better sense and understanding of what magical energy is. After all, the best and only real way to know magical energy is by actual experience. Here are the steps:

Be comfortable and relax. Close your eyes and relax. When it comes to manipulating magical energy, always remember that being relaxed is important as it will allow the energy to flow smoothly. Relax your body and your mind. Now is not the time to think about anything. In stillness and peace, there is great power and serenity.

Place your hands in front of you as if you were holding a ball, with the palms facing each other. Next, slowly move your hands apart — and as you do so, inhale slowly and deeply. Breathe through your nose. Next, slowly bring your hands together again as close as possible, but do not let them touch. As you move your hands together, exhale slowly. Continue this movement of the hands in sync with your breath. Be sure to synchronize the movement of your hands with your breath as this will naturally aid the flow of energy. Continue doing this for about three minutes.

Soon enough, you may start to feel something with your hands. The sensations may vary but usually appear in the form of heat, pressure, gravity, and a tingling sensation. Do not force yourself to feel something. Just keep your mind open and let go of everything. If you feel anything with your hands or between your hands, know that it is magical energy, also known as life force, that you are feeling.

The technique as discussed above naturally accumulates energy between the hands. This accumulation of energy becomes stronger and stronger to the point that you will be able to feel it physically.

If nothing happens on your first several attempts, do not be discouraged. Just keep on practicing, and you will surely achieve positive results soon.

Holy Cross Shield

The power of the holy cross is a potent protection against psychic attacks and negative energies. Fortunately, its power is something that you can summon at any time. You can cast holy crosses around you to keep away all negativity. The holy cross will be your shield of protection. Here are the steps:

Be comfortable and relax. Imagine four holy crosses around you: one in front, another at the back, and the other two one on each side. Hence, you will have one holy cross in front, at your back, and on your left and right side. The holy cross may look like anything that you want as long as it resembles a cross. It can also be as big as you want. Try to see it as clearly as you can in your mind.

The next step is to charge your holy cross with energy in order to make it powerful. To do this, imagine four rays of light descending from heaven. See and feel as these rays of light charge the holy crosses with divine energy, thereby making them powerful. Imagine the holy crosses lighting up as they become imbued and filled with divine energy. Continue this for as long as you like or until the holy crosses are fully charged with divine energy. When you are done, simply visualize the four rays of light fading away or returning back to heaven from which they came.

In order to further impress the purpose of the holy crosses, you can say an affirmation, such as, "These holy crosses protect me from all harm and negative energies. Amen." Repeat the affirmation two more times. Hence, overall, you will be saying the affirmation three times. When saying your affirmation, be sure to follow these basic rules:

- Keep it short and simple

- Make it clear and direct

- It should be in the present tense

- Say it at least three times

- Believe in whatever it is that you are affirming

After saying the affirmation, you can now go about your day knowing that you have a psychic shield that protects you from all harm.

It should be noted that all psychic shields require energy to survive and continue to do their function. On average, a shield created in the manner as aforesaid will last for about five hours. If you want to keep your shield for a longer period, then you should recharge it with magical energy from time to time. If a shield runs out of energy, it will disappear.

To recharge your shield with energy, you simply have to imagine it around you. Next, visualize again the ray of light from heaven and just let it recharge your shield just as when you first created the holy cross. Keep charging until all the four holy crosses are fully charged with energy. If it ever happens that you can no longer feel or sense your shield, it is possibly because it has run out of energy and has already disappeared. In this case, simply feel free to make a new one. After all, you can cast as many psychic shields as you want and as often as you want. Not to mention, the practice of casting a psychic shield will also develop your overall psychic and magical faculties.

Ray of Healing Light

We are now going to discuss another technique that may be of great interest to a magical practitioner. This magical technique is a potent healing technique. It uses a ray of healing light that comes from heaven. The power of this technique will depend on the skills of the caster. Hence, the more that you practice it, the more effective and powerful it will be. Here are the steps:

Assume a comfortable position and relax. Close your eyes and free the mind. When the mind is clear and in peace, magic simply overflows. Next, imagine a ray of brilliant white light descending from heaven. Know that this ray of light comes straight from the kingdom of God. It heals everything that it touches. See and feel as this ray of light enters your body through the crown of your head. Let it gradually fill you from head to toe. Feel its very powerful healing force. Be healed not only physically but also spiritually.

Do not rush the process of healing. Let it slowly fill you beginning from your head, down to your neck, chest, arms, hands, abdomen, waist, legs, and down to your feet. You should be able to imagine it by seeing and feeling it. Do not think of this as a mere fancy thought. With enough practice, you will actually feel its immense power — and you will know for certain that it is truly magical energy in action.

Keep absorbing more and more energy until you are satisfied. Once you are filled completely, simply imagine the ray of healing light either slowly fading away or returning back to heaven —

but be sure to keep all the healing energy that you have already absorbed in yourself.

It is also a good practice to pray the traditional *The Lord's Prayer (The Our Father)* as you do this healing technique. It may take some practice to apply this technique smoothly and effectively, but it is surely worth learning. Once you get used to it, you can even apply this technique in public and yet no one would even be able to notice it. Indeed, this is a very good magical practice, and it will also develop your skills in the art of manipulating magical energy.

Christian Mysticism is Not About Magical Power

It should be noted that gaining magical power is not the primary objective of Christian mysticism or Christian magic. Indeed, when you set out on this path, you will also gain psychic powers, as well as many other spiritual benefits. However, you must not allow yourself to be misled by mere magical prowess. Know that your main focus must always be on Jesus Christ. If you are able to fully unite yourself with Christ, no magical power can ever overcome you. You will also be able to do what many occult practitioners and masters could only dream of. This is because nothing will be impossible for you. If you are with Christ, nothing is impossible. In fact, miracles can be as natural as breathing.

When you engage in Christian magic, the practice of meditation is very much recommended. In fact, it can be said that it is even required. The practice of meditation will naturally develop your overall magical and spiritual faculties. This is usually how one acquires magical power. Still, always keep in mind that these powers are just a part of the path to Christ. If you allow yourself to be misled by these powers, you will not be able to reach your destination. Never keep your mind off of Christ, who is our Divine Master and God.

It is also good to note that there are many saints who did marvelous works of miracles without even engaging in any form of occult technique. An example of this would be Saint Padre Pio. Padre Pio is known to have prayed the Rosary more than

30 times a day. No wonder he did so many miracles. Actually, it was not really him who did the miracles, but it was God working through him. We must remain humble. Indeed, in humility, there is real power — for God loves the meek in heart.

Of course, gaining some powers along the way can be fun, but just do not allow yourself to be misdirected. It is very easy to be blinded by power. Therefore, we must remind ourselves with the teachings of Christ from time to time. This is another reason why daily reading of the scriptures (as contained in the Bible) is necessary. Always remember that all powers come from God. Instead of focusing on and seeking power, only seek Jesus, and you will never go wrong. But rather, your life will be overflowing with miracles.

On Sin

The subject of sin is a hot topic on Christianity. However, it should be noted that there are many ways one can approach this subject. Indeed, sin is real. But, what is sin? Sin is anything that is not in accordance with the will of God. It damages our relationship with the Almighty for every sin that we commit corrupts our soul. But, do not worry, Jesus has saved us from the effects of sin. As long as we believe in Him and follow Him, we can trust God that everything will be alright.

There are followers of Christ who take sin as a grave and serious matter, so much so that they worry too much about their sins and even spend hours being sorry for their sins. Although it is good to be sorry for our sins and to do our best not to commit any sin, it should be noted that focusing too much on sin is also not a good approach. But thinking about sin too much, we miss the path that we should be taking. Christ has commanded us to love, not to worry so much about sin. Do not forget that the state of our mind is also often the expression of our acts. If we focus too much on sin, then we might fail to love. Remember that our goal is not only to avoid sinning, but that we must also make our soul rise to be in union with Divinity. Simply not sinning alone is not enough.

There are those who take a miserable path beating themselves up for the sins that they have committed, but there are also those who move forward with Christ and start doing wonderful things instead of being too sorry for their sins. Personally, I like moving forward and enjoying life with Christ rather than feeling too sorry for my sins. Of course, I am sorry for all the sins that I have committed, but I believe that we are called for something much greater and meaningful than simply being sad and sorry. In the famous story of the adulterous woman, while the people were continuously condemning the woman who was caught in the very act of adultery, Jesus simply told her, "Go and sin no more." Indeed, Jesus wants to give us life (with so much divine love). Are we going to just stay and feel sorry all the time or are we going to move forward to a mysterious adventure with Christ? The choice is yours to make.

The Elements of Magic

In the practice of magic, there are four elements that you need to know: fire, water, air, and earth. These are the four elements of nature. It is believed that all things in the universe, visible and invisible, are made of at least one of these elements. It should be noted that the elements are not limited to their physical manifestation. This means that, for example, the element of fire is not limited to the physical fire as most people know it. But rather, from a pure magical perspective, these elements hold certain qualities. To help you understand this better, let us discuss them one by one:

Fire

The element of fire is said to be the very first element in creation. It is light and warmth. It has the following qualities and attributes: courage, war, lust, sex, the color red, determination, hotness, electric, strong will, the south direction, the head and especially the eyes, the magical creature known as salamanders, and everything that emits light, among others.

Water

It is said that there cannot be fire without the opposite force. In this case, it is the element of water. The element of water has the following qualities and attributes: beauty, healing, cleansing, magnetic, the west direction, the color blue, the magical creatures known as undines and mermaids, all bodies of water, the stomach, and the power of mediumship, among others.

Air

The element of air is another interesting element. However, in some magical traditions, they do not consider the air element as a pure element but somewhere in the middle of the fire and water element. Its attributes and qualities are as follows: the east direction, the magical creatures known as sylphs and all air faeries, communication, creative expression, movement, the color white or yellow, the chest region, travel, breathing, speed, and smooth action, among others.

Earth

Last but not least is the earth element. Again, in some magical traditions, they only consider two real and pure elements: fire and water, while air and earth are considered to be somewhere in between. Nevertheless, most magical practitioners consider all the four elements to be pure elements in and of themselves. Personally, I also share the view that they are all pure elements of nature and the universe. The Earth element is one of great interest since we, humans, are all creatures of the earth. The qualities and attributes of the earth element are as follows: the north direction, the magical creatures known as gnomes, dwarves and goblins, natural instinct, survival, strong foundation, stability, the color green or brown, the planet earth, the area of the waist and down to your feet, and the power of manifestation.

It should be noted that the aforesaid are just the general qualities of the elements. It is still the duty of the magical practitioner to get to know them one by one and see how the energy of every element merges and affects their own personal energy. The effects may vary from time to time. For example, a magician may consider the water element as the right and proper element for healing (which also happens to be a power that rightly belongs to the water element), but another magician may find that the fire element is more suitable for them for healing. Again, it also depends on how your own personal energy merges with the energy of the element concerned. Hence, get to know the elements one by one and see how their power combines with yours.

Get to Know the Elements

Getting to know the elements is easy. You just have to spend more time with them and be aware of their presence. Fortunately, every element has a manifestation and existence in the physical world. For example, let us say that you want to get to know the element of fire. To do this, spend more time in sunlight. You can also light a candle and meditate on the flame. The key is to get close to the element's representation in the physical world and expose yourself to it with the right awareness of the presence of the element and its energy. By doing so, you will be able to connect with any element of your choice and get to know it in a more intimate manner.

It should be noted that the elements are very much alive. They are not a neutral force. They have a spirit. Therefore, do not think that you are simply dealing with an inanimate object. It is worth noting that the elements are pure spirits of magic, so never underestimate any of them.

Let us say that you want to get to know the water element. In this case, you should spend more time with water. Take a shower and be more conscious of the water that touches and cleanses your body. This time, know that it is not just physical water that washes you, but that it has a water spirit which also contains energy. You can also take a bath in the rain or spend some time in the pool or even in the ocean. By exposing yourself to the power of water, you will be more connected to it. Do not try to control anything. Just be open and connect to the water element in the spirit level. Open your heart and mind, and you shall experience the beauty of water naturally.

The same principle if you want to get to know the air element. In this case, you can go outside and feel the breeze. Be conscious of it and be aware of the energy of the air. Take a deep breath and feel the air getting absorbed into your body. You can even imagine your whole being absorbing the energy of the air. Breathe and let the element of fire give you life.

Last but not least, let us say that you want to get close to the element of earth. You can go outside and spend more time in nature. You can also just stay in your room as you hold a natural rock or stone in your hand. If you do not have a stone, you can use a leaf or even a twig. By getting close to nature in whatever form you choose, you will be able to learn more about the earth element and establish a closer relationship with it.

Christian Magic with Elemental Application

Let us now put the power of the elements into actual application in a Christian way. Once you know the power of the elements and how they work in your life, you can tap their energy at any time to serve your purpose. For example, let us say that you want to be healed of something. By applying your elemental knowledge, you know that you can use the element of water. The only exception here is if you ever find a more suitable element than the water element. Still, most magical practitioners would agree that the water element is highly suitable for healing. In this case, here is something that you can do:

Imagine a holy cross above you. You may even imagine it floating in the sky. Now, see and feel that a waterfall made of holy water is descending from this holy cross and showering upon you. See and feel as the holy water touches you. See and feel the holy healing water entering your body and even into your soul. See and feel yourself shining brightly as you are getting filled with holy healing water coming from the holy cross. Continue for as long as you like. Do not rush the healing process. Spend as much time as you like. When you are done, thank Jesus Christ, and imagine the holy cross slowly fading back into the sky.

You can also use the said technique to heal another person. In this case, instead of being the one receiving the healing holy water, send it to the person who needs healing. See and feel the healing water charging and healing them.

Magic is an art. The technique that we have discussed is just one of the countless applications of elemental knowledge and magic. Do not be afraid to use your own creativity and make your own discoveries. After all, the path of magic is a path of discovery and enlightenment. Also, never forget that it is first and foremost spiritual. Therefore, its practice should help make you a better person with a soul that is full of peace and love.

Here is another example to help you better understand the application of elemental powers. Let us say that you are feeling afraid. You can conjure the element of fire with its power of courage to help you overcome the fear. To do this, you can slowly pray Psalm 23 as found in the Bible—and as you do, see and feel that you are shining brightly like the sun. See and feel yourself becoming empowered and shining brightly like the noon-day sun. Shine with power and might—knowing that you are with Christ. As you are doing this, you can also imagine Christ beside you, reassuring you that He is always with you.

You may think that this is just a simple use of the imagination. Indeed, it is a magical application of the imaginative power. In the practice of real magic, the imagination plays a very important role. The more that you get used to the use of the imagination, the more that you can develop your magical skills and abilities.

With regard to the development of the imaginative power, which is very important, the practice of imaginative prayer and/or the Alexandrian method of reading the Bible would be of significant help. Combine this with your ability to harness the elements of magic, and you shall be at the threshold where miracles and wonders abound.

It is also a recommended practice to be aware of the presence of the elements in your everyday life. This will also help you develop the magical sense—a psychic sense that connects you to the invisible world, the world of spirits—also known as the world of energy and pure magic.

Beware of the Modern World

As a magical practitioner, and especially as a follower of the Divine Master, you must beware of the modern world. The world is very tricky that it is very easy to get misdirected and lost in its many tricks and illusions. This is also another reason why the practice of meditation is important. Meditation frees the mind from all illusory things. It will naturally help you discover who you truly are. It will destroy all the man-made and falsified masks that blind us from reality. It always helps to take us back, helping us find our roots, our source—which is always being one with the Divine. Therefore, let us always make the practice of meditation a priority in our life.

The modern world also has its system that will corrupt you if you allow yourself to be absorbed by it. Be sure not to allow yourself to be controlled by the world. Always remember who you are, and never forget who you are. The world will do its best to change and corrupt you, but be of good courage and have faith. Never forget that our Lord and Savior, Jesus Christ, has overcome the world and all its evils. Christ is King. Christ is God.

You must learn to think for yourself. However, it is important to be sure that the mind is ready. How do you know that the mind is ready to think for itself? It is when the mind is one with the divine will. Therefore, it is important to read the Bible every now and then. These repeated readings of the Bible, over time, will naturally influence the mind. Once the mind absorbs all these teachings, most especially the teachings of Jesus, the mind will naturally have its own spiritual shift and renewal, turning itself into the mind of Christ.

There are many evils in this world. There are also many perverse teachings and practices. You must be on your guard, and be very careful not to allow this world to corrupt you. In this regard, it is a good practice to exercise a habit of self-introspection, especially when it comes to the thoughts that you keep and entertain in your mind, as well as how you live your life.

As a follower of Christ, know that you are not of this world. This world is, indeed, evil. You are only here for a brief period. It is too brief as compared to eternity in God's kingdom. This earthly realm is like your training ground. There will be sufferings, yes, there will be downfalls and disappointments, as well as many challenges, yes—but know that in all these, you can always be with Christ who is the source of life, and the only one who can give eternal life.

Examine your life if it is really the way that you want it. There are many people who are unaware that they are already being manipulated. Hence, it is good to stop and reflect on one's life as it is right now. Be sure that you are living in accordance with the teachings of the Divine Master, always.

On Following Christ

Never forget that we must always follow Jesus Christ, the Divine Master. Make it a daily practice to read the Bible, especially the teachings of Christ. Do not just read the words on face value, but we must also reflect on them. Now, reading is one thing, putting what you have learned into practice is another, for even the demons know the scriptures and yet fail to abide by its Spirit.

Once you know the teachings of Christ, you can already start following them. By abiding by the words of Christ, you will be following Him. Now, following Christ may not always be an easy duty. Of course, it is very easy to follow Him when things are all going your way, but what if things take a turn against your interests? In this case, it is important to have a clear view on what your real interest or objective is. Is it to follow your own will and plans or to follow Christ completely?

Once you realize that you are always with Christ, you must know that you are doing very well despite the present circumstances. To be sure of this, that you are abiding in Christ, you just have to abide by His words. As long as we are with Christ, we can be sure that we lack nothing, and that we can always be happy. It may take some time before one can reach this level of spirituality, but it is nonetheless doable, and you are the right person to do it. Do not worry, you will not be alone, for Christ will also help you achieve this level of spirituality.

Christ taught us that whoever wants to come after Him, they must deny themselves, take up their cross, and follow Him. The renunciation of self is an important teaching. We ought to renounce ourselves so that Christ can fill us with Himself, thereby elevating our soul to that of Divinity.

Now, following Christ and living with Him do not require anything of us except only ourselves. It does not matter what our personal circumstances are or how much money we have in the bank or what our race or religion may be. Remember: Christ is the God of all. Christ is for all.

It is said that those who truly follow Christ have nothing to worry in life. You have all the right to be happy because you are always with God. From now on, you must learn to Iive the spiritual life. The spiritual life is a life that does not depend on external things and events. It is a life within, a life of the soul, and a life with God. It remains unblemished by the world. Regardless of what happens to the world, even to your physical body, your spiritual life can continue to rejoice and be at peace.

Now, be careful from those who claim to be followers of Christ. Indeed, many people these days say that they follow Christ, but their actions show otherwise. Never be like them. Take note that there is a difference between those who believe in Christ and those who actually follow the footsteps of the Master. After all, even demons believe in Christ. As a true follower of Christ, we must not only believe, but we should also apply the teachings of Jesus in our daily life by putting the divine teachings into actual practice.

Following Christ is the daily duty of a Christian. This is also the way to have an intimate relationship with Him. It is also only by following Christ that one can attain the so-called Christ-connection. This is the kind of spiritual connection that you can have with Jesus. It is a divine connection where you can always be sure that God is always with you and is even within you. This kind of union with God is so intimate that no one can ever take it away from you.

Whenever you feel that your own self ego is interfering with your desire to do the will of God, always be humble. By being humble, the grace of God will fill you — and this grace of God will bless you with peace. It is a kind of peace that surpasses all understanding. Once you reach this level, you can always rest in God, for He is always with you, and He loves you tenderly beyond words.

Live by the Spirit

Living by the Spirit comes naturally when you do the will of God with your heart. The key is to let go of yourself. You must transcend your human state and unite with the energy and vibration of the Divine. You should free yourself from your body, even from the world.

In Christian magic, there are three divine virtues: faith, hope, and love. These virtues are also in the scriptures. In everything that you do, be aware if you have these virtues present in your life. These virtues emanate a certain vibration, which naturally raises the energy of man into something that is far more spiritual.

According to a saint, material things will never make us truly happy. No matter what we do, these things will never really satisfy us. It may give us some temporary pleasure, but it will just be brief and very much transient, and it is even difficult to depend on it. Material things will never make us truly happy because we are made in the image and likeness of God. As such, material things can never satisfy the soul. The only way the soul can rest and be happy is by elevating it, uniting it with the Divine. When the soul is one with Jesus, nothing will be impossible for you, and you can always rest in God, without fear, without worries. You will truly be free and happy.

From now on, think of yourself as what you really are: a soul. You are a soul that is merely having this human experience for some time. Hence, be sure to make it count by doing what is good and by always doing the will of Christ. The will of Christ is what is best for you. It is not that He is making you a slave, but He simply knows what is best for you. After all, He is the eternal God. Why would you listen to your own ego when God has already given you the way to truly live, which happens to be the way of Jesus. Hence, Jesus said, "I am the way, the truth, and the life." If we live by the words of Christ, then we shall be living by the Spirit.

On Letting Go

Once you develop a closer relationship with God, you may soon come to a point where you can freely let go of everything. By this time, you shall have realized that as long as you are with Christ, then that is all that matters. It may take some time for one to reach this level, but it is nonetheless doable.

Our life here on Earth is too limited. There is simply not enough time to do everything. But, we can still do something, and we can do it with love. This should be enough. Every act that is done with love is always holy and pure.

It is important that you take a good look at your life and be aware of how you spend your days. Be sure that you are making enough time for your spiritual needs.

The more that you let go of the parts of yourself that you do not really need, the more that you will be filled with divine grace. Many times, we prevent the work of God from happening in our life by blocking it with our own ego, will, and even our own expectations of what the Divine is. A better approach is simply to let go and relax. If you do this, you will be able to witness the magic of the universe unfolding right before you.

Let go and let God. If you learn this approach, there will be absolutely nothing that you need to worry about. You can enjoy at all times for you will no longer be dependent on what happens in this material world, for you will now be living a life in the spirit.

It must be clarified that this act of letting go is not something that you do that God can take advantage of. It is actually for your own good and benefit. You may not understand it right now, but you will surely be glad for it in the future. Jesus knows your past, present, in future. Trust Him and have faith all the time. You are not alone. Surrender everything to Christ, and you will be free.

There will be times when you will have to let go of things so that you can make time for what is truly important: your spiritual life. I know that this can be hard at times, but you must realize that there is ever really one thing that is necessary, and that is to be in union with Christ. When moments like this come, it is better to lean not on your own understanding. Instead, trust in the Lord with all your heart, and He shall soon reveal to you His wonders and everlasting love.

Self-Annihilation

The subject of self-annihilation is something that will arise once you develop a closer relationship with Christ. When Christ asks more of you, then you will soon enter into this phase of spiritual development. Self-annihilation is more difficult than mere letting go. This phase contemplates total destruction of the self. It may sound too drastic or even bad; however, it is an important step to a higher spiritual development.

Mystics who have reached a very high level of spirituality always have an encounter of this phase. It is a really difficult part of spiritual progress, but it is nonetheless achievable, and it is something that you can overcome. After all, even in this phase, although it may feel as if you have been abandoned by God, it is actually a moment of divine grace. It is also referred to by many as the *dark night of the soul*. It is a really difficult part of the journey akin to depression; but if you stay strong and get through, you will achieve a very high level of spiritual development. You will also gain wisdom, peace, and faith that is truly unshakeable.

This stage of magical and spiritual development will happen on its own. Once you are ready, then the Lord will send you this cross. However, do not think of it as if God were just punishing you and making you suffer just for nothing. He does not want you to suffer. But, this cross is important as it is the cross that will teach you and make your soul grow beautifully.

Do not worry, it is said that you will only receive this cross when you are ready. Therefore, if you do receive it, be happy about it. It also means that God has so much trust in you. However, it should be noted that most people who encounter this cross always feel like they could not carry it for it is such a heavy burden. Always remember that Christ is always with you, and this is true even during those times when you do not even feel or sense His presence. Have faith, be of good courage, for Jesus is always with you. Always. All ways.

Be Happy

There are various ways to Christian magic and mysticism. There are those who take the traditional and mainstream approach where they feel bad about their sins. However, there is another approach, and that is the way of happiness and love. In fact, there is a sect of Christian magicians and witches who take this more positive approach. With this approach, you celebrate life and every moment of it. Indeed, every moment is a celebration.

Still, regardless of the path that you take, know that Christ wants you to be happy. Of course, this does not mean that you can commit whatever sins that you want. Sins separate us from God, so we should never give sin power over us. But rather, by always being with Christ, there is always something to be happy about, as well as to give us peace.

Every moment is a moment of life. Every moment is also a moment that we can spend with Christ. As such, there is always something good to be happy about every time. Happiness is a choice, and you deserve to be happy. After all, Christ wants you to be happy.

There may come a time when you will be willing to relinquish all of your magical knowledge and powers just to give yourself fully to Jesus. When this happens, do not hesitate. In fact, so many saints who did not even have any occult training were able to do so many wonderful miracles simply by giving themselves completely to Christ. After all, once you are one with God, nothing shall be impossible for you, simply because nothing is impossible with God.

Have faith, be of good courage, and always do the will of Christ. From now on, make it a priority to have a close relationship with Christ, and happiness—true happiness—shall be yours, for Christ is the way, the truth, and the life, and He loves you without end.

About the Author

www.charlzdelacruz.com

Password to enter the private page: *ANGEL912*

Don't miss out!

Visit the website below and you can sign up to receive emails whenever Albertus Crowley publishes a new book. There's no charge and no obligation.

https://books2read.com/r/B-A-OUQJ-EBECC

BOOKS 2 READ

Connecting independent readers to independent writers.

Did you love *Basic Christian Magical Theories and Exercises*?
Then you should read *Solitary Sex Magick*[1] by Albertus
Crowley!

Solitary Sex Magick is an occult manual that teaches the
magical practice of sex magick.

This manual has been specially written and prepared for the
passionate solitary practitioner.

Since magical instructions are key to learning, this manual
has been modified into an easy-to-read format.

Sex magick is a pure magical science and art, and he/she who
learns its secrets shall discover real magical power.

1. https://books2read.com/u/3Lg5ww

2. https://books2read.com/u/3Lg5ww

Learn the foundation of the Craft of Magick and harness the forces of nature through solitary sex.

Why practice sex magick in solitary?

This is because it is actually hard to find someone to do it with.

Take note that you cannot just do it with anybody.

You have to understand that in the real practice of sex magick, there will be a merging of energies, as well as a merging of the souls.

If you end up practicing this craft with someone who has an impure soul, then you will only be corrupted, and the magic will not work.

Sex magick in the purest kind of magick as it originates from a raw instinct of man.

As such, you know that the energy that you harness is pure and of divine source.

What is more, the energy is not just any other energy, but the energy of life.

Humanity would not have continued to exist if the people did not engage in sex.

Sex is life and life is energy — and you can harness and manipulate this energy in a magical way.

Solitary Sex Magick is the key that will open wide a door of magick for you, and this door shall lead to many paths and magical experiences for you to explore and enjoy.

After all, the practice of magic ought to be experienced.

It is only through personal experience that you can fully understand the meaning of a technique or practice.

The same is true in the practice of sex magic (just like any other magical practices) — you ought to experience it yourself to realize its power.

Do not worry; the practice of solitary sex magic is highly pleasurable, so you would not have any problems with it.

In fact, you will even be comforted and brought to great heights of pleasures and ecstasy.

You will literally feel your body vibrating as it becomes filled with lots of magical energy, similar to the so-called full-body orgasm — only stronger and purer.

Your body shall throb like a heartbeat as it bathes in divine energy.

Are you ready to learn the secrets of this art form?

If yes, then let me now welcome you into the divine mysteries of sex, where you shall discover raw and potent power that you can harness for the realization of your will.

Always with love and with light, blessed be!

Read more at https://www.charlzdelacruz.com/.

Also by Albertus Crowley

Magick Unveiled
A Codex on Magical Energy
A Codex on Elemental Magick
A Codex on Power Meditation
A Codex on Spirit Communication
A Codex on True Energy Healing
A Codex on Pendulum Magick
A Codex on the Power of the Third Eye
A Codex on Energy Vampirism
A Codex on Sex Magick
A Codex on Making an Energy Ball
A Codex on Psychic Shielding Techniques
A Codex on Telekinesis Magic
A Codex on Auric Manipulation

Standalone
The Sorcerer's Training Manual
Astral Projection Manual for Beginners
The Monolith of Magical Practice

The Grimoire of Moloch
Solitary Sex Magick
The Inner Witchcraft of the Mind
Psi Ball Manual
The Christian Witch
Creating Words of Power and Affirmations
The Jesusism Spirituality and Way of Life
A Magical Course on the Pyramid of Magic
A Beginner's Guide to Ghost Hunting
Divination Using Ordinary Playing Cards
Manifestation Magick for Beginners
A Handbook on Wizardry
Dark Magic Manual
The Way of the Solitary Witch
Master the Craft of Magical Visualization
The Sorcerer's Handbook on Mind Magic
The Sorcerer's Manual
Basic Christian Magical Theories and Exercises

Watch for more at https://www.charlzdelacruz.com/.

Milton Keynes UK
Ingram Content Group UK Ltd.
UKHW011834300823
427775UK00001B/13